NAME YOUR EMOTIONS

SOMETIMES I FEEL EXCITED

by Jaclyn Jaycox

PEBBLE
a capstone imprint

Published by Pebble, an imprint of Capstone.
1710 Roe Crest Drive, North Mankato, Minnesota 56003
capstonepub.com

Library of Congress Cataloging-in-Publication Data
Names: Jaycox, Jaclyn, 1983- author.
Title: Sometimes I feel excited / Jaclyn Jaycox.
Description: North Mankato, Minnesota : Pebble, [2022] | Series: Name your emotions | Includes bibliographical references and index. | Audience: Ages 5-8 | Audience: Grades K-1 | Summary: "What does it mean to be excited? Everyone feels excited sometimes! Children will learn how to identify when they are excited and ways to manage their feelings. Large, vivid photos help illustrate what excitement looks like. A mindfulness activity will give kids an opportunity to explore their feelings"— Provided by publisher.
Identifiers: LCCN 2021029868 (print) | LCCN 2021029869 (ebook) | ISBN 9781663972378 (hardcover) | ISBN 9781666325874 (paperback) | ISBN 9781666325881 (pdf) | ISBN 9781666325904 (kindle edition)
Subjects: LCSH: Emotions in children—Juvenile literature. | Elation—Juvenile literature. | Enthusiasm—Juvenile literature. | Happiness—Juvenile literature.
Classification: LCC BF723.E6 J39 2022 (print) | LCC BF723.E6 (ebook) | DDC 155.4/1242—dc23
LC record available at https://lccn.loc.gov/2021029868
LC ebook record available at https://lccn.loc.gov/2021029869

Image Credits
Dreamstime: Marcos Calvo Mesa, 13; Shutterstock: aleks333, 17, AVAVA, 19, Color Symphony, Design Element, Distinctive Images, 5, Dragon Images, 14, fizkes, 11, Juice Dash, 6, Juriah Mosin, 7, karelnoppe, 10, Krakenimages.com, Cover, mihalec, 21, Monkey Business Images, 15, wavebreakmedia, 18, Zhukovskaya Olga, 9

Editorial Credits
Editor: Erika L. Shores; Designer: Dina Her; Media Researcher: Jo Miller; Production Specialist: Tori Abraham

All internet sites appearing in back matter were available and accurate when this book was sent to press.

Printed and bound in the USA. PO4608

TABLE OF CONTENTS

Words in **bold** are in the glossary.

WHAT IS EXCITEMENT?

You have always wanted a dog. You promised to feed it and take it on walks. You've begged and begged. But your parents always told you "no."

Today, your parents are taking you to the animal shelter. You are finally getting a dog! How do you think this would make you feel? You are probably feeling excited! Excitement is an **emotion**, or feeling.

WHAT DOES IT FEEL LIKE TO BE EXCITED?

What is something that makes you feel excited? Maybe your family is going on a trip. Or your grandparents are coming to visit. How does it feel?

Excitement can make you feel joyful.
Your heart beats fast. You might feel
like laughing or yelling. It can be hard
to stay calm. You may even want to
jump up and down!

USING YOUR SENSES

Everyone has five **senses**. People can touch, taste, and smell things. They can hear and see too. Your senses help you understand what's going on around you. They send messages to your brain. It's where emotions start.

Seeing snow fall can make you feel excited. You love sledding! Smelling a cake baking can make you excited. Your birthday is coming!

TALKING ABOUT YOUR FEELINGS

Being able to name your emotions is important. Sometimes it's hard to sort out your feelings. Talking about them can help. Tell someone you trust how you are feeling. They have probably felt the same way.

Some feelings, like excitement, can get really big. Talking about them can help you calm down. It can also be fun to share your excitement with others. It can make you feel closer to them.

UNDERSTANDING EXCITEMENT

You get excited when you are looking forward to something. You can also get excited when something good happens. If you score a goal in soccer, you probably feel excited. You want to win the game!

Excitement is a good emotion. It's also an **intense** emotion. It usually passes within minutes. It can tire you out if it lasts too long.

Feeling excited can be good for you.
Positive emotions make people happier.
You make better decisions. It's easier to
get along with others too.

Excitement can make you worry less. It gives you energy. You are bored less often. It makes you feel alive!

HANDLING YOUR FEELINGS

You know that excitement can be a strong emotion. It can be a fun feeling to have. But it's important to be able to control it. If you get too excited and can't stop running around, you could fall and hurt yourself. It helps to know some tricks to handle your feelings.

There are lots of things you can do to calm down. Take a little break. Go outside and get some fresh air. Take deep breaths. Go on a walk with your dog.

You can also read your favorite book.

Color a picture. Play a game with a friend.

Listen to some calming music.

MINDFULNESS ACTIVITY

Grab a blanket, head outside, and turn your attention to the sky! This fun activity will help you calm down in no time.

What You Do:

1. Lie down on your back and look at the sky.

2. How many clouds do you see? Can you find any that look like circles?
   How about squares?

3. Can you find one that looks like a dog?
   Or a dragon?

4. Do they change shape as they move?

GLOSSARY

emotion (i-MOH-shuhn)—a strong feeling; people have and show emotions such as happiness, sadness, fear, and excitement

intense (in-TENSS)—strong or extreme

positive (POS-i-tiv)—helpful or upbeat

sense (SENSS)—a way of knowing about your surroundings; hearing, smelling, touching, tasting, and sight are the five senses

READ MORE

Holmes, Kristy. *Feeling Excited*. New York: Greenhaven Publishing, 2019.

Jaycox, Jaclyn. *Sometimes I Feel Happy*. North Mankato, MN: Capstone Press, 2020.

INTERNET SITES

KidsHealth: Talking About Your Feelings

kidshealth.org/en/kids/talk-feelings.html

PBS Kids: Feelings Games

pbskids.org/games/feelings

INDEX

ABOUT THE AUTHOR

Jaclyn Jaycox is a children's book author and editor. When she's not writing, she loves reading and spending time with her family. She lives in southern Minnesota with her husband, two kids, and a spunky goldendoodle.